Ultimate Allegiance
The Subversive Nature of the Lord's Prayer

By Robert D. Cornwall

Energion Publications
P. O. Box 841
Gonzalez, FL 32560

www.energionpubs.com

2010

ISBN10: 1-893729-84-2
ISBN13: 978-1893729-84-1
Library of Congress Control Number: 2010942570

"Our Father which art in heaven,
Hallowed be thy name.
Thy kingdom come,
Thy will be done on earth, as it is in heaven.
Give us this day our daily bread.
And forgive us our debts, as we forgive our debtors.
And lead us not into temptation, but deliver us from evil:
For thine is the kingdom, and the power, and the glory, forever.
Amen."

Table of Contents

From the Editors

The Areopagus is a hill in Athens that was once the meeting place of a Greek council. Paul preached on that hill while visiting Athens, presenting the gospel to the Athenian council and converting one of them (Acts 17). It thus provides an excellent name for this series of booklets that examines important issues in understanding Christian beliefs and developing sound Christian practice. Each booklet is intentionally short – less than 80 pages in length – and provides an academically sound and biblically rooted examination of a particular question about doctrine or practice or an area of basic Christian belief.

The Areopagus series is orthodox in doctrine but not bound to the doctrinal statements of any denomination. It is both firm in conviction and irenic in tone. Authors have been chosen for their ability to understand a topic in depth and present it clearly.

Each book is rigorous in scholarship because we believe the church deserves no less. Yet the volumes are accessible in style as we also believe that there are many pastors and laypersons in the church who desire to think deeply and critically about the issues that confront the church today in its life and mission in the world.

In keeping with these convictions, the authors in this series are either professors who are also actively involved in ministry, pastors who have not only thought through the issues but whose ministry has been guided by their convictions, or laypersons whose faith and commitment to the lordship of Jesus Christ and his church have contributed to the Great Commission Jesus gave to all of his followers (Matt. 28:18-20).

The *Areopagus Critical Christian Issues* series is not only meant to help the church think differently. We hope that those who read its volumes will be different, for the gospel is about the transformation of the whole person – mind, heart, and soul.

We take the words of the apostle Paul seriously when he says to the Athenians that God "has fixed a day on which he will have the world judged in righteousness by a man whom he has appointed; and of this he has given assurance to all by raising him from the dead" (Acts 17:31).

Allan R. Bevere
David Alan Black
Editors

Acknowledgments

Every book is the product of a team of individuals. They may not have written the words or even be responsible for the content or production of the book, but each in his or her own way has influenced and helped craft the finished product.

In the case of this book, I must first thank the editors for this series, Allan R. Bevere and David Alan Black, for their willingness to welcome this contribution to a series that wrestles with critical theological issues. I'm especially appreciative that they have been willing to expand the notion of orthodoxy to include the musings of one whose theology is perhaps to the left of theirs. I'd also like to thank my publisher, Henry Neufeld, for his work on this project and for seeing that publishing can be a ministry as well as a business. Henry's ministry is to publish books that cross the broad middle of the Christian faith so as to broaden the conversation. Being that I come out of an ecumenical tradition, and have traveled a rather intricate pathway in my own spiritual journey, it is good to find a publishing home in that vast middle of the Christian faith. And as with my editors, I appreciate his willingness to include my perspective in this series of books. Finally, I offer a word of gratitude to Jerry Gladson, who carefully read through the text and provided needed and helpful guidance.

Because these reflections on the subversive nature of the Lord's Prayer began as a set of six sermons, I must extend a word of gratitude to the congregation who received these words and who have encouraged my ministry of writing. So, to the people of Central Woodward Christian Church, who graciously attended to the sermons, allowing me the freedom to develop my understanding of prayer, and this prayer in particular, even if they didn't agree at every point with my take on the subject, I extend this word of appreciation. I must add a word of thanks to the congregation for their willingness break with tradition, and instead of reciting the prayer, we sang it.

A final word goes to my wife Cheryl, whose love and encouragement has enabled me to pursue a ministry of writing over the length of our marriage.

Pentecost 2010

Preface

Prayer stands at the center of the Christian experience. At its simplest, prayer is a conversation between a human being and God, but surely it is more than this. Prayer, after all, takes a wide variety of forms, both simple and elaborate. While prayer has a vertical dimension, uniting human beings with the divine, it also has a horizontal dimension. As with the two great commandments, our prayers link us to God and to neighbor. If taken seriously, prayer is more than simply telling God what we humans want to have done on our behalf (or on the behalf of a friend or relative). It is a statement of trust and commitment, by which we declare our ultimate allegiance to the God who receives our prayers. There is something subversive about such a prayer, for it puts us in a position to engage the world in which we live in freedom from the ordinary constraints of culture. That kind of prayer can be empowering and world-changing, for it allows us to see things from a different perspective – a divine perspective.

Prayer that is subversive is prayer that engages "the powers that be." As Walter Wink puts it:

> Those who pray do so not merely because they believe certain intellectual propositions about prayer's value, but because the struggle to be human in the face of suprahuman Powers requires it. The act of praying is itself one of the indispensable means by which we engage the Powers. It is, in fact, that engagement at its most fundamental level, where their secret spell over us is broken and we are reestablished in a bit more of the freedom that is our birthright and potential (Wink, *The Powers that Be*, p. 181).

xi

Prayer is a foundational practice of the Christian faith, one that connects human beings to the one who holds our ultimate allegiance. Prayer allows us to respond to the Creator and Sustainer of the universe, who has invited us into a covenant relationship that transforms lives and worlds. As we do so, we join with Peter, who declared to the religious leaders of his day: "We must obey God rather than any human authority" (Acts 5:29). When we acknowledge our allegiance to God, we will find the source of our identity and the freedom to live lives that reflect that identity.

There is, for Christians, no clearer expression of this allegiance than the prayer that Jesus taught his disciples. It is a prayer that has been passed down from one generation to the next. For some it has provided a model prayer, and for others it is a prayer to recited, weekly and even daily. *The Didache* advised believers to recite it at least three times each day. Of course, it's possible that a prayer that gets recited this regularly can lose its value and meaning. It can, that is, become just words repeated as if by rote. And yet, the very durability over time of this particular prayer, brief as it is, suggests that these words transcend time and cultures, inviting each new generation to consider to whom they owe their allegiance, and in whom they find their purpose in life. Indeed, this prayer continues to be, for so many, the foundation upon which a relationship with the living God is built.

Therefore, as beautiful and inspiring as its words might be, the Lord's Prayer remains at its very essence a subversive prayer. It is a pledge of our allegiance to God, one that challenges our world views and our loyalties. It does so by connecting us with the one who empowers and guides us through life.

I approach this traditional but subversive prayer from a certain context. I serve as pastor of a Disciples of Christ congregation that prays this prayer each week, but then this was true as well of the Episcopal Church in which I grew up and first encountered the Christian faith. There was, however, a period in my life when I worshiped in less formal settings, in congregations that rarely if ever recited the prayer. These communities may have looked to the prayer for a model, but for these communities true prayer came from the heart and therefore it was to be extemporaneous. To pray one set of words, even if biblical, simply made no sense, and could even be seen as the precursor to the uttering of vain repetitions.

Perhaps it is a reflection of my own background that led me to reflect upon this prayer in the course of a series of sermons. I had begun to wonder what these words meant. If prayer leads to theology and to action, then what was it that I was praying? What did Jesus intend for his followers to take from this prayer? Having made the decision to focus on the Lord's Prayer, I laid out a series of six sermons. Each sermon lifted up one of the petitions that comprise the prayer, with a final sermon focusing on the doxology that closes out the traditional prayer shared in worship. Although this was a Lenten series, the final two sermons were preached on Palm Sunday and Easter, and thus reflected the events commemorated on these two hallowed days of the Christian year. The Palm Sunday sermon focused on the issue of temptation, which seems appropriate considering the context of Palm Sunday. The final sermon came on Easter Sunday, and it too seemed to fit nicely with the day in which it was preached. What better day to focus on a doxology than the day of Resurrection? The original context for those two sermons may not be as visible in these revisions, but it is helpful to know the background.

My hope is that this series of reflections will prove helpful to those who seek to deepen their own understanding of this prayer. For those readers who are preachers, perhaps this series will stir in their imagination the possibility of a similar series. It is possible that the reader will, like the author of this series, be surprised at what lies behind and between the words we recite. In my case, I discovered that the prayer of Jesus is much more politically focused than I expected — and I've read widely in books by John Dominic Crossan, Marcus Borg, and Richard Horsley, which lift up the political elements of the gospel stories. Nonetheless, the encounter with the prayer was insightful and challenging. It is my hope that the reader will also be challenged by what is found both here and in the prayer itself. May the reader find the prayer to be both spiritually enriching and deeply practical, whether the prayer is used as a model or one that is recited — from the heart — with great regularity, perhaps as often as recommended by the author of the *Didache*.

Introduction

The assumption of this book is that prayer has a subversive quality to it, because it upends the usual flow of our allegiances. Although God may be our creator, nation, family, clan, work, can all have greater influences on the way we live our lives. But because prayer, especially this prayer, calls for a sense of commitment to God, it directs our attention to a different way of life, one that reflects the reign of God. It is because prayer challenges rival claims of allegiance that it cannot be imposed by outside forces. It must come from one's inner convictions, or it will become nothing more than the meaningless repetitions that Jesus condemned in the Sermon on the Mount, a sermon that gives context to the prayer that Jesus taught his disciples (Matt. 6:7-8).

The prayer under consideration may be subversive in nature, a sense that suggests a certain political component, but there is another side to the prayer, one that recognizes our need to experience the presence of a transcendent but gracious God, one who reaches out to humanity out of love rather than out of a desire to manipulate or control. It is the assumption of this writer that the one to whom we offer our allegiance is not despotic or tyrannical, but rather one who desires what is best for the person who offers this prayer.

In Luke's Gospel we read that even as Jesus taught the disciples to recite this prayer, he also assured them that "everyone who asks receives, and everyone who searches finds, and for everyone who knocks, the door will be opened" (Matt. 7:8). God is like a parent who deeply loves one's child. If human parents won't offer a snake when the child asks for a fish, or a scorpion when an egg is requested, then surely the God who pours out the Spirit upon humanity will not act unjustly. God is gracious, merciful, and just

(Luke 11:9-13). To give allegiance to such a God doesn't require of us blind obedience. Instead, our allegiance is given in response to an invitation rather than due to any coercive force.

As has been noted earlier, Jesus taught what we call the Lord's Prayer to the disciples in response to their requests for guidance in such matters. Over time it has served as both a model for prayer and a prayer that is recited in its own right. It has the sense of a statement of allegiance and dependence, but it also issues forth in worship and praise. Having become so familiar to countless generations of Christians, much like the equally familiar Psalm 23, the prayer provides a comforting word of hope during difficult times. When no other words seem to issue forth, these words, words recited daily or weekly, can provide the link that sustains one's walk of faith.

As one who found great meaning in this prayer, John Calvin devoted considerable space to this prayer in his *Institutes of the Christian Religion*. Through this prayer, Calvin suggests that we are able to "acknowledge his boundless goodness and clemency." It gives expression to our own sense of need and desire in words appropriate to such a conversation between human and divine.

> For he warns us and urges us to seek him in our every need, as children are wont to take refuge in the protection of the parents whenever they are troubled with any anxiety. Besides this, since he saw that we did not even sufficiently perceive how straightened our poverty was, what it was fair to request, and what was profitable for us, he also provided for this ignorance of ours; and what had been lacking to our capacity he himself supplied and made sufficient from his own. For he prescribed a form for us in which he set forth as in a table all that he allows us to seek of him, all that is of benefit to us, all that we need ask. From this kindness of his we receive great fruit of consolation: that we know we are requesting nothing absurd, nothing strange or unseemly — in short, nothing

unacceptable to him — since we are asking almost in his own words (Calvin, *Institutes of the Christian Religion*, 3:20:34).

While Calvin acknowledged the spiritual utility of this prayer, he also recognized its distinctive beauty:

> Truly, no other can ever be found that equals this in perfection, much less surpasses it. Here nothing is left out that ought to be thought of in the praises of God, nothing ought to come into man's mind for his own welfare. And, indeed, it is so precisely framed that hope of attempting anything better is rightly taken away from all men (*Institutes*, 3:20:49).

As we contemplate the meaning of this prayer, it is appropriate to stop and recognize that the prayer itself has great beauty and even a perfection that can never be surpassed.

Even as this prayer possesses great beauty and even perfection, as it offers an appropriate means of sharing one's petitions with God, it also carries with it a sense of Jesus' understanding of the kingdom of God. This prayer finds its center in serving as a kingdom petition. As John Koenig puts it:

> The prayer that Jesus taught is among the shortest of the daily disciplines in the world's great religions. But to the eyes of Christian faith it shimmers like the most precious of diamonds. When we pray it, allowing ourselves to be centered in the kingdom petition, a prism effect occurs. With light from the Spirit, other parts of the prayer fan out into a rainbowlike display of what it means for us to participate in the coming reign of God (Koenig, *Rediscovering New Testament Prayer*, p. 48).

Each of the five declarations and petitions that form the prayer serve as affirmations of God's reign. They allow us to declare our allegiance to the God whose name is hallowed above all others, and then moves into petitions that direct and guide our daily lives, whether that be requests for daily provisions or relief from temptation.

Although there isn't space to delve deeply into the issue of the sources and editing of these two versions of the prayer, an issue that also includes the question of the way in which Jesus addresses God as Father, I would like to briefly comment on both the sources of what appears in the current texts and the meaning of the word father in this prayer.

The Lord's Prayer appears in two Gospels, Gospels that often make use of a collection of Jesus' sayings normally referred to as "Q." As is true with other sayings, each author uses the text in a way that fits their particular context and purpose. Matthew's version is much more expansive than Luke's, and provides the foundation for the forms that have been historically used in Christian worship. It is, however, impossible to determine which is closer to the original. What is perhaps most interesting is that Matthew chose to place it at the very center of the Sermon on the Mount.

With regard to the use of the word Father in this prayer, there has been considerable debate. In both passages the Greek word *pater* is used, but it is extremely likely that Jesus would have used the Aramaic *abba*. The debate concerns the way in which the Aramaic original influences the way in which the Greek word is used in this prayer, so that we might better understand what Jesus meant when he addressed God as Father. Although Jesus likely used the word *abba,* both authors chose to use the Greek word and no attempt was made to transliterate the Aramaic into Greek letters. We are, therefore, left with the decision made by the authors to use the Greek *pater.* The author/editors of these two Gospels could have used a transliteration, though the only example from the Gospels is Mark 14:36, an account of Jesus' prayer in the Garden of Gethsemane. The only other usages of the Aramaic term come in the Pauline epistles (Rom. 8:15; Gal. 4:6). The sparseness of this evidence would seem to suggest that it would be best not to speculate on the way in which the Aramaic word may have been used, and what its meaning would be.

The lack of evidence has not kept people from reflecting upon the word or making claims about the usage. Numerous books, both scholarly and popular, have suggested that not only did Jesus use the word *abba*, but that this word expressed an extraordinary sense of intimacy. Many interpreters have also suggested that such usage originated with Jesus — that is, while God may have been spoken of as Father in the Old Testament, God is not addressed directly in such terms. In their exploration of the meaning of the term, some writers suggested that the word *abba* is best translated as "daddy," and thus would have been the word a child used to address his or her father. Some even go as far as to suggest that the word has the sense of a toddler babbling "dadda." The acknowledged source for much of this speculation goes back to the writings of biblical scholar Joachim Jeremias, who indeed insisted that Jesus used the word *abba*, and at least originally held that it expressed the intimate expressions of a child to one's father. He apparently backtracked somewhat from some of these assertions. Now it is possible that Jesus spoke in intimate terms and that he used *abba* in the way Jeremias suggested, but there is simply no way to know this for sure. What we do know is that at least in terms of this prayer, the Gospels use the Greek *pater* and not the Aramaic *abba* (Thompson, *The Promise of the Father,* pp. 21-34). For the purposes of our study, I've focused on the implications that the word *pater* provides us, for it carries with it the sense of patron and thus emphasizes the nature of allegiance that I believe is present in this prayer.

What follows is a set of six reflections that is brought to a conclusion with an afterword that raises the question of what allegiance to God looks like as we live in the present age. Thus, we begin with a chapter entitled "Worshiping the Holy God." From this point, we move on to consider "Living in the Kingdom," "Trusting the Day to God," "Living in Forgiveness," "Deliverance from Evil," and finally, "Sharing in God's Glory." This final chapter reflects upon the closing doxology of the prayer: "For thine is the kingdom, the power, and the glory." This final statement doesn't appear in either of the two Gospel accounts, and thus is not original to the prayer, but it is so much a part of our prayer that it is appropriate that we not neglect it in this set of reflections. In many ways, without this statement, the prayer comes to an abrupt ending, leaving us wanting more. It would appear that early on this lack was noticed and a proper ending was provided.

Chapter One
Worshiping the Holy God
(Our Father who art in Heaven)
Isaiah 6:1-8

We worship a holy and loving God. These two images — holy and loving — may seem an odd combination in the minds of many. The word holiness elicits in our minds puritanical and separatist images. Don't eat; don't touch; don't look. There are many people for whom such images hold much meaning. God is in the minds of many a stern task master, demanding much and giving little. The word "father," which opens the prayer, often takes on much the same sense — especially in earlier generations, fathers could be distant and concerned about behavior. Thus, the idea that God is a "holy father" seems to fit well with our preconceptions. Love, on the other hand, carries with it a gentler, endearing, intimate sense. A father who is loving and compassionate is going to be forgiving and less concerned about holiness. The biblical witness, however, speaks of God both in terms of holiness and love, and therefore we must reconcile them with each other if we are to understand who this Father is whom Jesus addresses in the prayer he taught his disciples.

The prayer itself, as recorded in Matthew and Luke, invokes the holiness of the Father, inviting us to not only affirm God's holiness, but it requests that God make God's name holy on earth as it is made holy in heaven. Love may be present in this prayer, but Jesus begins with holiness. It is in light of this address to the holy God, who is our Father, that we can understand the nature of God's reign and our place in God's realm.

PRAYING A KINGDOM PRAYER

In Matthew's account of the prayer, its introduction comes in the midst of a broader discussion of the nature of God's kingdom. In the course of teaching his audience what it means to live faithfully in the kingdom, he introduces the matter of prayer. He tells them not to pray like the hypocrites, who stand in places of worship or on street corners, reciting prayers more designed to attract attention to the prayer's piety than to the one being addressed in the prayer. In contrast to these hypocrites, Jesus suggests that his disciples would be better served by seeking out a secret place, where they could offer prayers that represent a true conversation with the creator of heaven and earth. Not only should they seek a secret place for their prayers, but they should also remember that it's not the quantity of words that gets God's attention. As Jesus reminds them, God already knows their needs before they ever ask a thing of God (Matthew 6:5-8). In approaching this God, whose name is being hallowed on earth and in heaven, it is appropriate to remember that prayer isn't designed to impress God or one's neighbor. Eloquence is not the key ingredient in kingdom prayers; rather it is persistence and humility.

Having offered these warnings, Jesus turns to his audience and proposes a new model for prayer. Pray like this, he suggests — and then he begins with these simple words that have been recited by countless generations of Christians: "Our Father, who art in Heaven; hallowed be thy name." In this opening line of a brief but powerful prayer, the believer is invited to come before God with humility to share in a life-changing conversation with the one who reigns over all.

OUR FATHER

Jesus' kingdom prayer begins with an invitation to address God simply as "Our Father." So powerful is this statement that the Roman Catholic tradition has chosen it to be the title of its version of the prayer. Each of these two words — "our" and "Father" — has implications for one's faith journey, and both words in this opening phrase have great importance.

The first word, "our," suggests that Jesus intends us to understand this to be a corporate prayer and not a private/personal one. It is true that Luke's version doesn't include the word "our," but the decision made by the church down through the centuries to follow Matthew's lead is important to note. Too often we envision the faith journey as being a lonely and individual pathway. It's just me and Jesus, alone together on the road. It is a sensibility that fits well with the modern desire for spirituality without religion. For many this spirituality is not only eclectic, but it is extremely individualistic, allowing little room for community to develop. But if we are to address God in the fashion suggested by Jesus, using the word "our," then we will hear a very different witness. As each of us takes our journey down the road of life, it is not just me and God, but it is God together with the community that takes the journey with me.

There is a second implication to the use of "our" in this prayer. Remember that Jesus invites us to pray this prayer *with him*, so in essence by teaching the disciples this prayer, which begins with "*our* Father," Jesus issues an invitation to join him in God's family. That is, when Jesus invites us to pray to "our Father," he includes himself in this statement. He may be a son by descent, but we are children of God by adoption, and it is in this sense that God is our Father. John Calvin picks up on this in his meditation on the prayer. He reminds us that in praying this prayer as God's children, we offer prayers to one who can be trusted. He writes:

> By the great sweetness of this name he frees us from all distrust, since no greater feeling of love can be found elsewhere than in the Father. Therefore he could not attest his own boundless love toward us with any surer proof than the fact that we are called "children of God" (1 John 3:1; Calvin, *Institutes,* 3:20:36).

Therefore, we pray this prayer corporately, as children of God who share jointly in Jesus' own relationship with God the Father.

The second word in this prayer requires even more thought and unpacking. It's likely that most people who pray this prayer have a certain sense of what the word "father" means. They may also have a sense of what this term of address means for them, which can be either positive or negative. For instance, if you've had a positive relationship with your father, then you might have a positive sense about the word. But, if you've had a negative experience with your father — whether he was abusive or distant or simply not present — then you might have a different feeling about the word.

In our day, there is an additional issue that needs to be kept in mind — the question of gender. What for instance does the fact that we are addressing God in masculine terms signal to both men and women about equality in church and society? If God is male, as the title suggests, then are men superior to women? If God transcends gender, then is it appropriate to edit the prayer and pray to God as our Mother? These are important questions that require our attention because they relate to our understanding of justice and equality.

Because this prayer has such a storied place in our liturgy we find it difficult to modify any aspect of the language used in the prayer, so much so that we continue to use words like "hallowed" and "art" and "thy," even if we wouldn't use the words any place else in the liturgy. So modifying the prayer to make it more modern and egalitarian is difficult. Since it is such an integral part of the prayer, it is important that we try to understand what the word "Father" meant to the people Jesus taught the prayer.

Although it is possible, perhaps even likely, that Jesus used the Aramaic word *abba* in addressing God, the word that is used for the Father in the two Gospel accounts of the Lord's Prayer is the Greek word *pater*. That fact should be taken into account as interpreters seek to understand the meaning of this statement, especially when it comes to speculations as to the possible meanings that the word *abba* might carry. As we saw in the introduction, some interpreters have suggested that Jesus' alleged usage of *abba* carries with it a sense of intimacy that would have been novel, perhaps even carrying with it the sense of "daddy." This usage is very tempting, because it appeals to our desire to share in an intimate relationship with God. Indeed, I myself desire such a relationship, one that is deeply personal and intimate, especially since my relationship with my own father, who is now deceased, was anything but close or intimate. To read this into the prayer, however, requires a degree of speculation that might not be warranted. What we have before us is the Greek word, and it carries a different sense of relationship. One needn't reject the idea of intimacy, but one should be careful how this interpretation is used.

If we start with the word that is in the text, *pater,* and then try to understand what the original readers might have thought when they read it, what would they have understood Jesus to be teaching them? It would be helpful to note that the word *pater* provides the root for such words as patriarch and patron. Considering the rest of the prayer, and the fact that Jesus sets it in his teaching on the kingdom of God, we might want to think in terms of a patron or sponsor. Such an idea would reflect well Jesus' own context. To get a sense of what is happening here you might want to watch one of those old epic Roman movies, like *Ben Hur.* In that movie, Judah Ben Hur, a Jewish prince, is enslaved on a Roman galley. When he saves the life of the commander of the ship, Judah first becomes a gladiator, and then later is freed and made son and heir of the Roman commander by adoption. What we learn in this film is that one needn't be born into a family to have all the rights and responsibilities of a member of the household. By his own decision, the Roman noble, Arius, adopts Judah Ben Hur, who takes the name Arius and calls the Roman his father.

To push the image further and perhaps even closer to the context of the prayer, in the Roman world the Emperor was considered the Great Father of the people. So, one could say that in addressing God as Father, the early Christians were signaling that their ultimate allegiance was to God and not the emperor. In making this reference to God, we get a sense of the subversiveness in the prayer. That is not to say that there is in this prayer a call to active revolt, but rather that obedience to the emperor or the state was tempered by the teachings of the faith. The emperor may be the temporal ruler, but for Christians there was only one patron or sponsor, and that was God; the God who had adopted them into the household. So, as we pray this prayer, we are forced to ask the question: To whom do I owe my allegiance? Is it God or is it nation, family, or some other identity?

We see this sense of adoption present in Paul's letter to the Romans, where he suggests that having been freed from the spirit of slavery we can now cry out "Abba Father," because the Spirit is speaking through us giving witness to our adoption as children of God. Yes, it would appear that Paul emphasizes this relationship by combining the Aramaic *abba* with the Greek *pater*, to emphasize this change in status. Therefore, when we address God as our Father — recognizing the gender related problems inherent in that confession — we give thanks that God has adopted us into the family, making us "heirs of God and joint heirs with Christ" (Rom. 8:15-18). Whatever promises are made to Jesus, our elder brother, are made to us, and we can receive them in trust, knowing that God's love for us is infinite in character and breadth. Therefore, we need not be anxious about anything (Phil. 4:6).

HOLY IS YOUR NAME

From our initial address of God as "Our Father," we turn to the first petition of the prayer. The focus of this first petition is the holiness of God. Jesus invites us to ask that God's name would be hallowed, or made holy in our lives. This petition reflects the commandment that was given to the people of Israel at Sinai:

> You shall not make wrongful use of the name of the LORD your God, for the LORD will not acquit anyone who misuses his name (Deut. 5:11).

The commandment speaks of respect, reverence, and honor, and this sense is present as well in Jesus' teaching on prayer. Perhaps this is why Jesus tells his audience to pray in secret and not think that the wordiness of their prayers would impress God (Matt. 6:5-8). Both the commandment and the instructions remind us that as we pray our focus is directed toward God and not toward ourselves.

This sense of holiness and awesomeness, which is present in the prayer, is lifted up in Reginald Heber's great hymn of the faith, "Holy, Holy, Holy!" This hymn reflects the heavenly worship described in Isaiah 6:1-8 and again in Revelation 4:8-11, calling us forth to rise early in the morning and declare our allegiance to the God who is merciful and mighty, and to whom we bow in worship.

To get a sense of what is meant by the phrase "holy is your name," it is helpful to turn to Isaiah 6. There we find the prophet feeling overwhelmed by his vision of God's throne. As the prophet envisions the heavenly scene, the only thing that is on his mind is his own feelings of being unworthy to stand before God, or as the hymn puts it, only God is holy, and whatever holiness we might attain to is derivative of our experience of God's grace.

As we consider the prayer and the meaning of these words, the phrase "holy is your name" helps qualify our sense of what it means to be in relationship with God. While I believe that God desires to be in an intimate relationship with us that expresses the love that is God, this relationship is also rooted in God's holiness. Consider that, when appearing to Moses in Sinai in the form of a burning bush, God said to Moses:

> "Come no closer! Remove the sandals from your feet,
> for the place in which you are standing is holy ground"
> (Ex. 3:4-5).

Not only is the heavenly realm holy, but since God dwells among us, the very ground we tread is holy ground. It is, as Michael Crosby, a Catholic priest, puts it:

> If God's name is going to be made holy on earth as it
> is in heaven, the consecration of God's presence or

name must begin in the ground of our being. In the power of this name everything in our house — be it at the individual, interpersonal, and infrastructural level — must be honored; everything that profanes that name must be resisted. Such is the task of those who belong to the household of that God whose holy name is revealed in the I Am (Crosby, *The Prayer that Jesus Taught Us,* pp. 61-62)

God's name is made holy, not just in our words, but in our very lives. It is for this reason that, even though our relationship with God might be intimate in nature, it isn't one of equals, lest we seek to take advantage of God's name and profane that name in the way we live.

With the prophet, we may my cry out to God, seeking God's mercy and forgiveness, so that we might live anew this petition that God's name might be hallowed in our lives. And if God's name is made holy, then with the prophet we may experience great joy and find our calling in life. With this as our starting point, we can continue the journey through this prayer, contemplating its meaning for our lives.

Chapter Two
Living in the Kingdom
Thy Kingdom Come
Luke 13:18-21

We live in a modern democracy that enshrines the words:

> We the People of the United States, in order to form a more perfect Union, establish Justice, insure domestic Tranquility, provide for the common defense, promote the general Welfare, and secure the Blessings of Liberty to ourselves and our Posterity, do ordain and establish this Constitution for the United States of America.

The nation's founders threw off a ruler in order to gain independence from a faraway king, and yet, week after week, we pray that God's kingdom would be revealed. As we offer this prayer that God's kingdom would be revealed, we also ask that the will of God be done, on earth as it is being done in heaven. It is almost as if we were asking for help to do the king's will on one side of the Atlantic, even as it was being done on the other side. With our political identity wrapped up in ideas about democracy and freedom, how do we reconcile our prayers with our politics?

We could try to reconcile these two very different political ideologies — democracy and monarchy -- by spiritualizing the kingdom of God. Since we live in a democracy here on earth, we get to run our own lives in the "here and now." Then, when we get to heaven, God can be in charge! Unfortunately, Jesus doesn't let us off the hook so easily. We might imagine that Matthew's use of the phrase "kingdom of heaven" in place of "kingdom of God" allows for a bifurcation between earthly and heavenly realms, as if this kingdom stuff applies to the next life, but the way the kingdom is described in the prayer — especially in Matthew's version —

doesn't allow for this interpretation (see Crossan, *God and Empire*, pp. 116-117).

The prayer, as Matthew presents it, asks that God's kingdom would come, as God's will is done on earth as it is done in heaven. What happens on earth, Jesus suggests, mirrors what is happening in the heavens. It would seem that as we make this prayer to God, we are recognizing that with the incarnation, the kingdom of God has taken root in this world. As Jesus puts it, the kingdom is in our midst. It is, as Jesus puts it in the Gospel of Luke:

> The kingdom of God is not coming with things that can be observed; nor will they say, "Look, here it is!" or "There it is!" For in fact, the kingdom of God is among you (Luke 17:20-21).

Now, I should point out that many translations replace the word "among" with "within." If we go with "within," then it is easier to spiritualize the kingdom message, so that it's just a matter of me and Jesus having a "personal relationship" until I get to heaven. When we think in these terms then the kingdom doesn't have any social or political ramifications. But, if the kingdom of God is all around us, even if it's invisible to the naked eye, then the message is quite different.

THE KINGDOM — THE HEART OF THE PRAYER

If we believe that the kingdom of God is more than getting into the next life, so that the kingdom has "this world" implications, then what is it that we're requesting of God? What is the nature of this kingdom that we're asking God to reveal in our midst? As we consider these questions, it's important to remember that the kingdom isn't a minor focus. It is instead the focus of Jesus' ministry. Everything he did, whether he was teaching or healing, revealed to the world the nature of God's reign. Therefore, it shouldn't surprise us that this petition stands at the very heart of this prayer. Everything that is lifted up in this prayer is rooted in the premise that the kingdom of the Holy God is now present and is being revealed in the ministry of Jesus. This includes our request for God's daily provisions as well as requests for forgiveness and protection against the inroads of evil. All of this is rooted in the assumption that God's kingdom is truly present in the here and now.

Now, when we pray this prayer, we need to be aware that there are other kingdoms that have a claim on our allegiance, just as they did when Jesus taught this prayer to a people living under Roman occupation. As I pointed out in the previous chapter, the Roman emperor considered himself the Great Father, and the people of the empire were his children. He promised to provide them with bread and protection in exchange for their absolute obedience and worship. So, when Jesus invites us to pray this prayer, we need to remember that God's kingdom stands in contrast to Caesar's — whether Caesar is an emperor or a president doesn't matter. It is because the early Christians understood themselves to be living in a parallel culture or kingdom that they were considered a threat to Roman society. In their minds, their primary allegiance was given to God — as Peter declares in his appearance before the Sanhedrin. "We must obey God rather than human authority," (Acts 5:29).

The kingdom of God is, as John Dominic Crossan notes, the "standard expression for what I have been calling the Great Divine Cleanup of this world. It was what this world would look like if and when God sat on Caesar's throne, or if and when God lived in Antipas' palace" (Crossan, *God and Empire*, pp. 116-117). In Crossan's mind, this kingdom of God is fully religious or spiritual and political. It is a call to transformation of the world in which we live. It may seem to be a utopian vision, one that has no possibility of fulfillment, but the ways of God are not our ways. The kingdom comes not with sword or *coup d'état*. It is not a party ideology — whether of left or right. But if God is to reign on earth as in heaven, then we cannot separate the spiritual and the social.

The word politics might seem too secular for us, but what about the word justice? It seems to be part of Jesus' understanding of the kingdom. N.T. Wright notes that for him the term justice is "a shorthand for the intention of God, expressed from Genesis to Revelation, to set the world right — a plan gloriously fulfilled in Jesus Christ, supremely in his resurrection (following his victory over the powers of evil and death on the cross), and now to be implemented in the world." In his understanding of justice he rejects a dualism that believes nothing can be done about the situation on earth prior to the return of Christ. Instead, without going back to the old Social Gospel (which had many good elements in it), we should think of ourselves living "consciously between the resurrection of Jesus in the past and the making of God's new word in the future." In response to those who think that an emphasis on the resurrection reinforces the old dualism, he writes that it is because "Jesus Christ rose from the dead, God's new world has already broken in to the present and Christian work for justice in the present, for instance, in the ongoing campaigns for debt remission and ecological responsibility, take the shape they do" (Wright, *Surprised by Hope,* p. 213).

As we contemplate what the kingdom looks like now and in the future, as well as the role that we play in its expansion requires that we recognize that God is the one who ultimately brings it into existence. That being said, it doesn't mean that we do not participate in this effort. It may mean sharing our faith, but it also means participating in a work that expresses God's presence in the world, transforming it into the vision that God has for this world.

In our efforts to discern what this prayer requires of us, even as we ask God to bring it into existence, it is helpful to give heed to Jesus' parables. Time after time, Jesus will tell a story or make a brief statement that begins with the words "the kingdom of God is like. . . ." Therefore, as we consider what it means to pray this prayer, asking that God's kingdom would be revealed in our midst, then the meaning of this revelation will be found in parables like the one Jesus tells about mustard seeds and the one he tells about yeast.

SMALL IS BEAUTIFUL

The first of these two parables of the kingdom in Luke 13 speaks of the mustard seed. According to the parable this is among the smallest of all seeds. It's so small that it's difficult to even see it, and yet the promise of a very large mature plant is present in that seed. I expect that when Jesus says that the kingdom is in your midst, his audience was likely looking around, wondering what they should be looking for. After all, they couldn't see a throne or an army. All they could see was a rag tag band of Galileans following a rather young religious teacher. Where is the kingdom?

The good news that is present in this parable is the reminder that small is beautiful. Now, that's not a message that's easily heard, whether in the broader culture or in the church. And yet, the message of the parable is quite simple — big things can have small beginnings. As one commentator suggested, the people expected the kingdom to be like a mighty cedar, like the one promised in Ezekiel, but as Luke reminds us, Jesus' ministry was similar to that of the mustard seed. It's full of promise, but we can't see the fullness of its presence just yet. But when it does arrive in its fullness, it'll be much like that cedar. It will grow large enough to host the birds of the air in its branches, just as the prophet suggested (Ez. 17:22-23; Culpepper, "Gospel of Luke," *NIB*, 9:275-276).

That promise of nesting space has been interpreted to mean inclusion of Gentiles into the people of God, and of course in the broader scope of the gospel message, that is part of the story. But, it also carries with it the sense that the kingdom provides a home, a place of rest and safety. It is, to paraphrase Augustine, the place where the heart finds its rest.

The parable calls for us to change the way we envision a kingdom. We equate kingdoms with spectacles or demonstrations of power. Whether the ruler was David, Solomon, Herod, or Caesar, all of them resorted to their might, their ability to overcome their foes. But this isn't the model of God's reign present in the parable. God will bring about God's purpose, but it will happen in a very different way.

A community of faith need not be rich and powerful by human standards to make a difference. Hearing this can be difficult, because our culture tells us something different. It tells us that riches and resources are required to change things. Money talks, after all! This can be even harder to hear for churches. To live out the reign of God is to embrace the call to be a missional presence in the communities in which we live. It won't be wealth and power that will determine success. Instead, it will be our willingness to allow God to use us for the transformation of the world.

A LITTLE IS A LOT

In case one parable isn't sufficient to make the point, Luke adds a second parable. This parable speaks of yeast, though it might be better to speak of leaven. The image here is that of a small ball of fermented dough. When added to fresh dough or flour starts the leavening process. In this case, a woman hides a small amount of leaven in three measures of flour. That may not sound like much at first, but consider that these three measures equal fifty pounds. That's enough dough to feed one hundred and fifty people, which makes for a lot of bread!

As we think about what this parable means for us, it might be helpful to remember that the words leaven and yeast were often used as metaphors for uncleanness and corrupting influences. For instance, Paul speaks of a little leaven corrupting a whole batch of dough (Galatians 5:9). Then there's the accounts in Matthew and Mark where Jesus warns the disciples about the leaven of the Pharisees and the Sadducees (Matt. 16:5-12; Mark 8:14-21). In all of these cases, yeast and leaven carry negative connotations. In this parable, the negative is turned into a positive. Although the leaven may work in much the same way, it leads to a different outcome. Instead of being a source of evil, it becomes a source of good.

As with the parable of the mustard seed, this parable underscores the power of smallness. It is a reminder to the early Christian community that while it might have been small in number, and its influence on society may have been initially quite limited, over time that little bit of leaven, hidden in the flour, would produce a lot of loaves of bread. The kingdom of God, therefore, may seem hidden, but it can change the dynamics of the world's existence.

What is the message here for the church of our day? Could it be that if we're willing to be signs of God's reign, both in our words and in our deeds, as well as in the way we interact with others and live our lives in the world, then we could be change agents in society? The question here is: in what ways are we yeast? In answer to these questions, we could suggest a few possibilities. We live at a time of great uncertainty and insecurity, when the tone of our nation's conversation is becoming increasingly polarized and angry. The community of faith, as it seeks to be agents of the kingdom, can change the tone of the conversation in society. It can also change the focus of our culture's attention away from spectacle, greed, and the search for power. That is, after all, what yeast does — it changes things. Paul writes to the Corinthian church and tells them that God has reconciled them in Christ, making them new creations, and therefore God was entrusting to them the message of reconciliation (2 Cor. 5:16-21).

To push this further, since we live at a time when the air of our culture is heavy with fear, mistrust, anxiety, and even great anger, the kingdom message calls forth a commitment to seek the common good. As Walter Brueggemann speaks of the faith community's journey toward the common good, he points us back to the Exodus story. In that story we see a people move out of slavery in Egypt to the freedom of Sinai. He makes a point that I think speaks to our situation.

> Those who are living in anxiety and fear, most especially fear of scarcity, have not time or energy for the common good (Brueggemann, *Common Good,* p. 7).

The message of the kingdom is this: we no longer need to live in anxiety. We need not fear scarcity, for we live in the midst of God's abundance. This is because the leaven is hidden in the dough. Indeed, as the next petition reminds us — God is the great provider. Too often we miss the signs of God's kingdom because we're too focused on living in Pharaoh's kingdom or Caesar's kingdom. And in that kingdom, there's never enough. That's because no one shares, and no one looks out for the other. It's a matter of everyone looking out for themselves. Such a description of reality is as fitting today as it was two thousand or three thousand years ago. That we should be concerned about the welfare of our neighbor seems to stand against the prevailing wisdom of the day.

In God's kingdom, however, things are different. In this vision of reality, the people of God are called upon to be agents of change, agents of transformation, and agents of reconciliation. The process of change and transformation begins with the community that we call church. If we're not reconciled — if love doesn't permeate this community or we spend our time grumbling about little things — then we'll find it difficult to answer the call to bear witness to God's presence in the world.

As we pray this prayer, asking that God's kingdom would be revealed in our midst, let's remember that this promised reign of God starts small — in a mustard seed and in a ball of fermented dough. The kingdom of God is not always visible to the naked eye, because it does not come into existence with all the trappings of power and might. There are no armies or thrones to be seen. And yet the kingdom is both coming and is present — now and forever more.

God has issued an invitation to us. If we're willing to listen and respond, we have the opportunity to share in extending the reign of God on earth, even as it is being extended in heaven. Yes, we have a choice to make, a decision as to whether we'll respond favorably to God's call on our lives. If we choose to participate in God's reign, we're committing ourselves to do God's will on earth as in heaven, and therefore engaging in the mission of God. This mission sends God's people out into the neighborhoods and communities with a vision that touches lives, brings transformation, and brings healing to one's neighbors and one's neighborhoods. The kingdom, after all, isn't simply about individuals. It's also about systems, networks, and communities. Indeed, the kingdom is like a social network through which God is reaching into our world and transforming it, just as yeast transforms dough.

Although referring to a different prayer — Jesus' high priestly prayer of John 17, Dwight Friesen speaks of the transforming nature of relationships in terms of "we'ing." The kingdom of God is an "open *We*" in which "the people of God are not a hermetically sealed group of holy men and women who stand apart from culture or society." Instead, he suggests that "our new networked identity as a people is to be a blessing to others, like yeast worked through dough, like a cluster of blessing in the complexity of a city" (Friesen, *Thy Kingdom Connected,* p. 55). The kingdom starts small, like a mustard seed or yeast, but as it spreads it transforms everything it touches. As we participate in this network of the kingdom, we participate in God's transforming work of grace in the world.

Chapter Three
Trusting the Day to God
Give Us this Daily Bread
Luke 12:22-34

The petition, "Give us this day our daily bread," follows upon the previous two petitions in the Lord's Prayer. The first petition requests that God would hallow God's name and then in the second petition we request God's kingdom and thus God's will to be done here on earth, just as it is being done in heaven. Our ability to make this request stems from our relationship to the holy God, who is our patron and sponsor. In making this request, we are trusting the day to God's care. In structuring the prayer as he did, Jesus mirrors the structure of the Ten Commandments, which also begin with acknowledging God's reign and then move to questions of human existence and behavior.

In making this petition, the petitioners acknowledge their dependence on God, which as we'll see involves saying no to Caesar's claim on one's life. This petition also stands as a recognition that before any other request can be made, we must attend to the most basic of our human needs — the provision of our daily bread. It is, as psychiatrist Abraham Maslow suggested, until our physiological needs are met, we can't deal with anything else — and that may include our attention to the things of God. As we consider this request for God to provide for daily bread, we might want to expand the definition to include all the basics — food, water, and shelter.

This request has its roots in the Exodus story, where the people of Israel find themselves wandering in the desert of Sinai without having sufficient supplies for the journey. Reading the Exodus story, one might think that this people expected theirs would be a quick trip across the desert. The story is instructive, because it reminds us that the journey of faith is not quick and easy. It's not just a hop, skip, and a jump — one day we're living in slavery and the next we're experiencing the good life in the Promised Land. The expectation is not surprising, for humans seem to want immediate gratification and solutions. This is very true today, in an age of microwaves and text-messages, but as the story reminds us, this isn't a new situation.

It isn't just the desire for instant gratification, however, that emerges from the story. It is again a reminder that there are basic human needs that need to be met, if we are to proceed with our engagement with the things of God. In this story, when the people realized that their trip would last longer than they expected, and finding themselves in a desert, which isn't the greatest storehouse of food and drink, they began to cry out to God, just as they had while in slavery. In their minds, living in slavery was bad, but dying of starvation and thirst while wandering in a desert was even worse. It should be acknowledged that these cries to God came mostly in the form of complaints and grumbling.

Once again, God hears their cries, and provides for their needs. God does this with a daily provision of quail, manna from heaven, and water from a rock. The provisions of God came with a few strings attached. The people were to gather the manna, which fell like dew on the desert floor, each morning. They could bake it or boil it, maybe even fry it, but they couldn't save it. If they tried to keep leftovers, the food would spoil by morning, so there was no reason to give into the human temptation to hoard. When they first saw the food, they rejoiced. Their lives had been spared. But as is often the case, it didn't take long for them to get bored with the menu. After a few weeks of eating nothing but quail and manna, they were ready for something new. Not only that, but they quickly tired of life in the desert. Once again they began complaining and grumbling (Ex. 16-17).

It's true that the people of Israel took a great risk in following Moses into the desert. Life may have been bad under Pharaoh's rule, but at least they knew what to expect. As we all know, sometimes what we know appears to be better than what we don't. So, facing the possibility of starvation in the desert may have made slavery look like a pretty good alternative. To continue the journey in the desert meant walking by faith and depending on God's provisions. The difficulty that this request entails is underscored by the story of the Golden Calf. When Moses didn't return from the mountain, the people got worried, but rather than put their trust in the God who called them out of Egypt and gave them manna and water, they made a Golden Calf and looked to it, for salvation (Ex. 32). We are tempted, as was true of the Hebrews, to turn to other gods, but in this prayer and in this petition Jesus reminds us of from whence our help will come.

DEPENDENCY ON GOD THE PROVIDER

In making this petition we come face to face with the one who is our provider, and we make this request: "Give us this day, our daily bread." This request is, in its very essence, a statement of faith in God. We're declaring our trust that God will provide for our basic needs. In doing this, we're also declaring our willingness to entrust the day to God's care. This subverts both a sense of self-reliance and reliance on Pharaoh and Caesar. This isn't to say that government might not have a role in providing a safety net for citizens and residents, but it is a reminder that God is ultimately the one who provides, and it is to him that we declare our allegiance.

Although the Exodus story stands behind this prayer, so do other stories that Jesus' disciples knew all too well. Those who were first taught this prayer lived under Roman occupation, and therefore they understood that Caesar, not God, was their great provider. Indeed, Caesar used bread, and when the bread ran short, he used circuses to control the mob. The point that Caesar liked to make was that the people's lives depended on his grace. Therefore, once again we find Jesus challenging the common wisdom, pointing us beyond the powers and principalities, to the one who truly cared for their needs. Jesus reminds us that it is God, the one we address as Father, who is our patron. Therefore, we are God's clients and not Caesar's, which means that we owe our ultimate allegiance to God and not to Caesar. This isn't necessarily an anti-government statement. One can believe in a robust role for the government in providing support for the people without making the state ultimate.

There is more to this petition than simply acknowledging God's patronage over Caesar's, as important as this is to our physical, mental, and spiritual well being. As Michael Crosby points out, in making this petition we're recognizing that we are not self-sufficient. For many of us this may be a more difficult issue to confront than allegiance to Caesar — for there is in our psyche, especially in the American psyche, the idea that we must take care of ourselves. When we take this attitude, an attitude that the prayer itself refutes, we're declaring our independence from both God and from neighbor. Crosby writes of the importance to his own spiritual life of realizing that he had "fallen for the original temptation of the serpent: to 'become like God'" (Crosby, *The Prayer that Jesus Taught Us*, p. 123). When we fall prey to this temptation, then God's daily bread becomes "our 'bread,'" which leads us to believe that we can provide for ourselves. At that point, our daily bread is no longer seen as a gift of God, and when we reach this conclusion then it's likely that we'll conclude that we have no need to share bread with others.

The problem that emerges when we conclude that everything is under our control, when we believe that we're in the driver's seat of life, is that we often fall victim to the dangerous mix of anxiety and fear. Anxiety can lead us to build protective fences that effectively shield us from the concerns and needs of our neighbors. It also cuts us off from experiencing the grace of community. It's at this point, when we're hanging on by a thread, that we hear Jesus say to us: What benefit does worry bring you? Does it add even a single hour to your life? If not, then why do you keep striving for food and drink, as the nations do? Does God not know what you need? Does God really care more for the ravens than for you? And yet, they don't seem to worry (Luke 12:22-34; cf. Matt. 6:19-21, 25-34).

OUR SOLIDARITY AS NEIGHBORS

If this petition is our "Declaration of Dependence" on God, it's also a statement of solidarity with our neighbors. One of the powerful messages of this prayer is that it is a communal statement. This is seen in the use of the pronouns "us" and "our." If, as is commonly done, we pray the Lord's Prayer as if we're using the first-person singular, then we have prayed in a way that is different from the way Jesus taught the prayer. Thus, we are called upon to pray: "Give us this day *our* daily bread." By using these plural pronouns in the prayer, we identify ourselves with our neighbors. When we pray this prayer, asking God's provision of our basic needs, our prayer levels the social playing field. Indeed, even those who appear to be our clients in life are, like us, God's clients. To pray this prayer faithfully requires a certain amount of humility.

Praying that God would provide manna from heaven also involves a willingness to share our bounty with our table mates. I think it's instructive that Jesus tells a prospective follower that he should sell his possessions and give them as alms to the poor and that it is easier for a camel to get through the eye of a needle than it will be for the rich to enter the kingdom of God (Luke 18:18-28; Matt. 19:16-30; Mark 10:17-31). There is also the description we find in the book of Acts of a community of faith that pooled its resources and shared with each other, so that no one was in need (Acts 4:32-37). These stand out as radical demands upon us, demands that Christians have rarely embraced. There have been the few, mostly those called to monastic life, who have embraced this call, but their numbers are not many. We celebrate St. Francis's decision to leave behind his inheritance, but we're not sure if this applies to us. Indeed, I'm not sure what to make of the radicalness of this demand.

Having not taken up the life of poverty, I must struggle with the demands of discipleship. It may be that only some among us are called to this life, but the prayer itself reminds us of our connectedness to the other. Thus, in praying this prayer we respond to what Walter Brueggemann calls the "practice of neighborhood." It's a commitment to pursue the common good, a recognition that simply because I don't make use of a particular service in society, doesn't mean that my neighbor doesn't. If we take into consideration the needs of our neighbors, then it may change dramatically the way in which we respond to a whole range of issues, from health care to unemployment, education to gay marriage. It is a matter of looking at the world through the eyes of one's neighbor, guided by the grace of God. As Brueggemann puts it, it's a movement "from scarcity through abundance to neighborhood" (Brueggemann, Common Good, pp. 30-31).

The biblical message is not one of "God helps those who help themselves." That phrase is more reflective of Benjamin Franklin than of Jesus. The message of neighborly solidarity may be best summarized by these words from Ecclesiastes.

> Two are better than one, because they have a good
> reward for their toil. For if they fall, one will lift up
> the other; but woe to one who is alone and falls and
> does not have another to help. . . . And though one
> might prevail against another, two will withstand one.
> A threefold cord is not quickly broken" (Eccl. 4:9-12).

RESTING IN THE PROVIDER'S GRACE

Jesus tells us to strive for the kingdom, and when we do so then everything else will follow in its wake, for it is God's good pleasure to give us the kingdom. All that is required of us is a willingness to receive God's provision as a gift of grace. So, don't worry about tomorrow. Instead, put your trust in God, for God is faithful. Such wisdom, of course, cuts against the grain of a common wisdom that we can depend only upon our own devices. Trust no one, but yourself; depend on no one but yourself. For some among us, life has left so many scars that such wisdom makes sense, but for most among us this belief system has been passed on from one generation to the next and reinforced by the culture. Unfortunately, such wisdom runs counter to the needs of community.

In Luke's Gospel, just prior to his statements about worry, Jesus tells the parable of the rich fool. In this parable, a rich man builds a barn to hold his grain. With a barn full of grain, he can now sit back and eat, drink, and be merry. He has reached the pinnacle of the American dream — he has no need for anyone else, because he's built a sufficient nest egg to last a lifetime. Alas, on that very night, this man dies (Luke 13-21). So who benefitted from this act of hoarding? And so it is, Jesus says, with those who store up treasures for themselves but are not rich toward God (Luke 12:13-21). Yes, and "where your treasure is, there your heart will be also" (Luke 12:34). And so the question is put to the reader: Where is your heart? On whom shall you depend? To pray this prayer faithfully requires an acknowledgment that one's help and sustenance comes from God.

Honesty requires us to acknowledge that we all hedge our bets. Pensions, savings accounts, and insurance — these are all prudent investments. Indeed, wisdom seems to suggest that we should plan for the future. Unfortunately, this "wisdom" too often leads to anxiety. That is because we have come to believe that everything rests on us. That is why we hoard.

As we struggle with the meaning of this prayer for our own lives, as we recite the words of this stanza of the prayer — "Give us this day our daily bread" — we confess our belief that God is faithful and gracious and loving. This God will provide all our needs, for as the third stanza of the hymn Amazing Grace puts it:

> Through many dangers, toils, and snares,
> I have already come;
> 'Tis grace hath brought me safe thus far,
> and grace will lead me home.

By acknowledging this reality, by affirming our dependence on God, we place ourselves in a position to look out for the needs of the other. By recognizing our dependence on God, we recognize as well that we are dependent on those whom God has placed in our lives.

Chapter Four
Living in Forgiveness
Forgive Us
Matthew 6:7-15; Luke 6:37-42

It's not easy refraining from judgment of others. We're quick to tell others "don't judge," but then just as quickly we find ourselves serving as both judge and jury. It could be the clothes one wears or the car one drives. It might be the politics or the religious ideology that causes us to engage in judgment. We love the fact that Jesus said "don't judge, lest you be judged," but we all find it difficult to remove the log that sits there in our own eyes, even as we try to pick out the speck in the eye of the other. In making these points Jesus raised the ongoing problem of self-righteousness, a problem well illustrated in the story of the woman caught in adultery. There may be textual issues to contend with, but the point is well taken — those without sin should cast the first stones. In this story, instead of casting stones, Jesus offers forgiveness (John 8:1-11).

Very consistently Jesus challenged the pretensions of those who claimed the right to judge, exposing their self-righteousness, and offering forgiveness as the foundation for life in the kingdom of God.

DEBTS, SINS, AND TRESPASSES

In our English versions and translations of the prayer, congregations may use one of three variants when describing that for which they're seeking forgiveness. God is asked, depending on the version of the prayer that is used by a congregation, to forgive one's debts, sins, or trespasses. Each of these words has its own meanings and nuances. By understanding these nuances we can better understand what it is that we're asking for in our prayers. We could ask which of these words is correct, but since the two versions found in the Gospels use different words, then perhaps it is best to affirm the validity and value of all three versions.

The two Gospel accounts, Matthew and Luke, use different Greek words. In Matthew the word used speaks of debts, while Luke uses one that can be best translated as sin. Although the other word, trespass, lacks biblical support it too has implications for understanding the prayer's meaning.

To start with Luke, the Greek word used here is *hamartia*. This is, in contrast to Matthew's usage, theological language. It speaks of falling short of God's expectations or breaking divine laws. When we think of sins, we think of our relationship with God and the ways in which we break God's laws. But if God is forgiving us our sins, as we forgive those who sin against us — how would another person sin against us? Could it be words spoken in anger? Slurs against the character of another? Gossip? Perhaps, our understanding of Jesus' usage here is illuminated by looking to the words of an earlier teacher, the Wisdom of Sirach:

> Forgive your neighbor the wrong he has done, and then
> your sins will be pardoned when you pray (Sirach 28:2).

Although the words of Sirach seem more conditional than do those of Jesus, both suggest that our own condition is related to how we deal with the other. Once again, we hear the communal nature of this prayer, which subverts our sense of self-sufficiency or, at the very least, the individualism of our spiritual experiences of God (Culpepper, "The Gospel of Luke," 9:235).

Matthew's use of the word debts (*opheilēmata* — Greek), suggests economic implications or perhaps questions of loyalty. It could be said that, at least in regard to God, we stand indebted to God for all that we are and all that we have as human beings. This would include our own identity, which comes to us as a gift of God. If this is true, then we owe God our loyalty, our gratitude, our very lives. But how do we forgive the debts owed to us? In thinking about this question, the situation in Haiti seems illustrative.

Here is a nation that has lived in deep poverty from the day of its birth. Then a natural disaster, in the form of a massive earthquake, added to the nation's already overwhelming misery. Even as people from around the world, including thousands of church people, contributed to its relief, questions were raised as to how a country could find itself in such dire straits. Reading the history of Haiti, one discovers that the nation had mortgaged its future simply to break free from French rule. Over time, due in part to embargoes and poor leadership, the nation's debts continued to grow. As a result, it had to give away even more of its natural resources in order to pay this accumulating debt. At this point in time, it would seem that the only way for this country to break free of its misery is for the debt-holding nations to follow the injunction of this prayer and forgive its debt. To forgive a debt is to set another free.

One need not go to Haiti to find examples close to home. As I write this, the United States (along with much of the world) is facing a severe financial crisis. There are untold numbers of people, good law-abiding and honest people, who find themselves no longer able to pay their mortgages or owing far more on their mortgage than their homes are now worth. As a result, many are simply walking away from their homes, leaving the homes and their investments in the hands of the banks. The issue of debt has significant implications for people of faith. If we have been forgiven our debts by a gracious God, how should we handle the debts of those who are indebted to us?

The use of the word trespass seems to have little textual support, but it remains a favorite rendering for many. This word, though it may have its origins in William Tyndale's translation of Matthew 6:12 and appears in the *Book of Common Prayer*, fits with the subversive nature of the prayer. If we take the word in its modern sense, to trespass is to cross boundaries and invade spaces. If the word is used in the context of this prayer, then we must consider the ways in which one might commit a trespass against God? If it has a sense that differs from sin, could it be that one commits a trespass when one takes on roles and duties that belong to God? That is, could we trespass against God by taking on such responsibilities as being a judge? Isn't God alone able to judge without malice? As for the manner in which we might trespass against our neighbors (or they against us), this might include such invasive practices as coercing people into the faith.

THE QUESTION OF RECIPROCITY

The way in which Jesus lays out this stanza of the prayer, suggests that forgiveness involves reciprocity. It's likely that we read this prayer through the filter of Paul's message of grace, and thus divine forgiveness is supposed to be unconditional. God's grace comes prior to any request on our part for forgiveness, and yet this prayer suggests otherwise. The words we recite suggest that God will forgive our debts in the same manner that we forgive our debtors. God's forgiveness may stand at the beginning of the process, but it seems that God expects something of us in return.

To understand Jesus' intentions here, one might look at the parable of the "unforgiving servant" (or official). As Jesus tells it, a king calls in the debts owed to him, but one official owes a sum that might have been unimaginable before Bernie Madoff came on the scene. It was such a large sum that this official could not have paid it off. With nothing to lose, the official begs the king for mercy, and the king, who is compassionate, takes pity on the man and forgives the debt in full. The official, who owed more than could ever be repaid, is now debt-free. And he went out of the palace courts leaping with joy — at least until he ran into a fellow official who owed him a great sum. Now this man's debts were nothing compared to what the first official owed the king. So you'd think that the one who was forgiven would return the favor. But that's not how things worked out. Instead, the one who had been forgiven demanded payment in full — immediately. When the other asked for more time, he responded by having the man thrown in jail until the debt could be paid. When the king, who had shown mercy on the man, heard this, he was furious that the man had presumed upon his mercy but wouldn't show mercy to another. And so we read that the man is to be tortured until he can pay the debt — and Jesus adds that the same judgment awaits those who presume upon God's mercy and don't show it to their neighbors (Matt. 18:23-35).

The sense of this stanza is a reminder that God's grace is costly grace. In making this point, Jesus suggests that our patron, the one to whom all things are owed, is willing to forgive us everything that is owed by us, but God also expects us to treat our neighbors in the same way. Therefore, when we forgive the debts, sins, and trespasses of another, we are acting as agents of God's divine forgiveness. What we owe God may be spiritual in nature, but what we owe each other is likely to be much more material in nature. As we pray the prayer, let us consider its implications for the economic realities that impinge on our lives. We might even ask whether this prayer is calling us to push our government to enact legislation that would free our neighbors — whether individuals or even nations — from unwieldy burdens?

FORGIVENESS AND RESTORATION

I will not pretend that this is an easy thing to do. It's one thing to receive God's word of forgiveness, and another to offer forgiveness to one who has offended or hurt us. Forgiving financial debts might be easier. Sometimes the hurt runs so deep that not only can we not forget, but cannot forgive. To hear Jesus say that our own forgiveness is contingent upon our forgiving others can be rather disheartening. We want to walk with God, and even be good neighbors who are committed to the common good, but this idea of contingency doesn't sound like good news. Another contingency, one found in Luke 17, places the question of repentance into the conversation. Jesus seems to suggest that if someone repents, one should forgive, even if that person comes back and repents seven times in a day (Luke 17:1-4). Although we are called to forgive others, so that we might be forgiven, the offer of that forgiveness seems to require some form of willingness to turn one's life around and begin a new direction — even if one continually stumbles along the way.

Ultimately, the only way for this to become good news is for us to remember what Jesus told Peter, when Peter asked how many times he should forgive the one who offended him. Jesus said, forgive as often as requested, even up to seventy-seven times (Matt. 18:22). Our hope is found in God's willingness to have us continually seeking forgiveness. As we do this, as we pursue God's forgiveness, then we can see God begin to transform our lives. By praying this prayer from the heart each week, each day, we acknowledge God's forgiveness and grace, and seek to offer it to those who need our forgiveness.

To forgive, however, means more than saying "I forgive you." Instead, it requires a willingness to restore the other to wholeness. Remember that Jesus teaches this prayer in a culture that is deeply rooted in traditions of honor and shame. Forgiveness generally involves finding a way for the other to save face. For us, this means allowing the one who has offended us to return to the prior status of neighbor.

FROM THE HEART

Finally, if we're to fully pray this petition, then it would behoove us to consider the word that concludes the parable. It is a command to forgive from the heart. In the cultural context in which Jesus makes this statement, it means that forgiveness involves our whole being, including both our emotions and our intellect. Forgiveness comes forth from the depths of our being, so that we might restore others, even as we are being restored and transformed. Each of us must, therefore, reflect on those relationships that are currently broken and discern what is required of us by this petition. This has implications for our personal lives and our public lives — including, I would suggest, the way we spend our money, vote, drive our cars, and more. Again, this isn't an easy thing to do, but we can go forth on this journey, knowing that we stand in the midst of God's grace. It is that grace that enables us to pray this prayer from the depths of our being.

Chapter Five
Deliverance from Evil
Deliver Us from Evil
Luke 4:1-15

As we come to the final petition of the prayer — as it is found in the two Gospels — we hear Jesus speak of temptation and deliverance. It is a petition that finds its roots in Jesus' own experience of temptation in the wilderness. According to the Gospels, immediately after the baptism by John, the Spirit leads Jesus into the desert. There he fasts for forty days and forty nights. By the end of this sojourn in the wilderness, he is hungry and thirsty, weak, and vulnerable. It's at this moment that the devil shows up and presents Jesus with three tests. On the surface, these tests don't seem all that evil, and yet they're designed to appeal to human weakness and desire.

Consider the first temptation — turning stones into bread. If you're hungry and it's in your power to provide yourself with relief, then why not do it? The second temptation is an offer of power, which is an important commodity if one wishes to accomplish something in life. All that is required of Jesus is that he provide the tempter with a bit of reverence and allegiance. Finally, the devil takes Jesus to the pinnacle of the Temple and reminds him that people like spectacles. So, why not jump and let the angels rescue him? That will get a crowd and a following. In each case, Jesus rejects the temptation, rooting his answers in scripture.

This desert experience served to prepare Jesus for the events that came at the end of his life journey. Consider the Palm Sunday story. The people offer him a crown, but he resists their offer to lead their revolt against Rome. Instead of picking up arms, he resists both empire and temple through his preaching — though he understood full well that by proclaiming to the people the message of the kingdom he placed himself in great danger. He could try to harness the energies of the people who sought a violent solution to their problem, but he understood both the futility of such an attempt as well as the fact that it ran counter to the message of God's kingdom. God's reign is, after all, a parallel culture that comes into existence not with political power or military might. Instead, the means to this end is the cross. As the Gospels make so very clear, Palm Sunday did not define in any real way Jesus' mission. It was a mere twist in a path that would lead to a confrontation with the powers that be, a confrontation that lead to death.

TEMPTATION: BASIC ASSUMPTIONS

As we consider this petition, which asks God to refrain from leading us into temptation, it's important that we consider a couple of basic assumptions. First, we should note that according to the scriptures, God can neither be tempted nor can God tempt anyone else (James 1:12-16). To do anything different would be to act contrary to God's very being as one who is good and loving. For God to do that which is evil would be to act completely contrary to God's nature. Furthermore, if anyone were to suggest that we should do what is evil in the name of God, then either these individuals have misheard God or they are simply misrepresenting God.

If the first assumption pertains to the nature of God as one who is incapable of doing evil, then the second assumption pertains to the person of Jesus. The promise found in the book of Hebrews, a promise that is designed to give us hope, states that while Jesus has been tested in all things, even as we have been tested, he remains without sin (Heb. 4:14-16). Although highly controversial, the movie *The Last Temptation of Christ*, together with the book upon which it is based, does us a favor, for it reminds us that in his humanity, Jesus experienced the same kinds of temptations as do we — whether they be sexual, political, or simply the desire for peace and quiet. Indeed, the final temptation in the movie involves Jesus climbing off the cross so he might take up a normal life with a wife and kids. Such a possibility would be a welcome temptation to many, and yet Jesus seems to have understood that his calling required him to stay the course. Therefore, he stays on the cross (this is true even in the movie, where in the end the temptation is understood to have been a dream).

Jesus' experiences with temptation remind us that God isn't in the business of pulling us out of any and every tempting situation or from every form of danger — remember, God did not rescue Jesus from the cross. At the same time, this text suggests that in Jesus we have an example of one who lived in complete fellowship with God and did not break allegiance, even though he experienced enticements as great as or greater than any of us have experienced, and he understood from his own experience the reality of evil. It was very much present in his midst. Therefore, in Jesus we encounter the parallel culture that is God's kingdom, a different way of living that stands apart from all evil.

FACING TEMPTATION

Having laid out these basic assumptions about temptation, then what is Jesus suggesting in this petition? What is the proper context to understand temptation in this context?   Many scholars would answer this question by suggesting that Jesus is speaking in apocalyptic terms. That is, in this prayer that Jesus teaches us, we are asking God to keep us from having to endure that final day of testing that comes at the end of the age, a time when good and evil collide in catastrophic ways. Help us, we pray, so that we might avoid such a day (Boring and Craddock, *People's New Testament Commentary*, p. 37). But if this petition only carries an apocalyptic sense, one that almost seems escapist, then the petition doesn't seem to connect with our daily lives. This is especially true if we're to understand this prayer to be culturally and socially subversive.

Although Jesus might have seen this prayer in apocalyptic ways, we might benefit by looking at the way in which James understood testing. Even as he insisted that God cannot tempt others to do evil or succumb to such a temptation, he also suggested that faith can be strengthened in the midst of testing. Is that not part of the message of the story of the temptation in the wilderness? Yes, Jesus experienced weakness as a result of the extreme measures of his fast, which made him vulnerable to the tempter's requests, and yet he did not succumb. James suggests that faith is strengthened when it's tested, even if God is not the tester.

Athletes understand what it means to be tested, as do musicians and even writers. You have to go through difficulties and challenges if you're going to improve your performance. As James puts it: "Know that the testing of your faith produces endurance; and let endurance have its full effect, so that you may be mature and complete, lacking in nothing" (James 1:2-4). Knowing that God, who is good, won't tempt us to do evil, then our prayer becomes a statement of trust in God's leadership, especially when we read this petition in light of Jesus' words about worry. Later in the Sermon on the Mount Jesus tells us not to worry like the Gentiles, who say: "'What will we eat?' or 'What will we drink?' or 'What will we wear?'" Instead, Jesus says, seek, above all else, God's kingdom (Matt. 6:25-33).

In mentioning food, drink, and clothing Jesus speaks to some of our biggest concerns in life. These also speak to some of the temptations that we face — especially temptations rooted in consumerism and narcissism. Every day, we're bombarded with enticements to buy this or that item that promises to make our lives easier and better. Whether we're watching TV, reading the papers and magazines, listening to the radio or checking the internet, or even as we walk the aisles of Costco or Walmart, we hear voices calling out to us: Eat this, wear this, drink this, do this, and you'll be happy. And if we don't really have a need, advertisers know how to create one within us. When consumerism is paired with narcissism, the message is: Buy this, because you deserve it! You are number one, and it's important that you take care of number one — even if that means stepping on your neighbor!

This prayer becomes culturally and socially subversive when it becomes the foundation for discernment. There will be many temptations, many opportunities to give allegiance to others, and often the choices won't be starkly black and white, good or evil. The choices often seem benign. To walk with God, to live out God's reign, means not taking the bait, but continuing the journey even when the journey becomes difficult.

DELIVERANCE FROM EVIL

The second half of the petition is absent from Luke's version of the Lord's Prayer, but it may be the key to our understanding the intent behind this petition. Although we begin by asking God to carry us through the time of testing, we conclude by asking God to deliver us from the evil one. That is, we ask that God would deliver us from the clutches of the one who seeks to encourage us to act contrary to God's will.

Before we look at Jesus' definition of evil, it would be helpful to think about the nature of deliverance. And, lest our imaginations get the better of us, I don't believe Jesus has exorcisms in mind — like the ones portrayed in famous movies. Deliverance from evil requires that one put one's trust in God rather than in the evil one. If we make the assumption that God is good and will not tempt us to do evil, then the way to put aside evil is to discern God's will and direction. This is what we do when we pray that God's kingdom would come and that we would do God's will on earth as it is being done in heaven. Ultimately, our deliverance is found in adhering to the two commandments that summarize the law and the prophets — that we should love God and love our neighbor. Everything that is good flows from these two commandments. If we attend to these commandments, then we shall be delivered from the evil one, for as the first letter of John puts it, "all who obey his commandments abide in him, and he abides in them" (1 John 3:23-

24). Indeed, to attend to these commandments is to follow the lead of Christ and walk in his ways.

The way of deliverance involves our committing our lives and futures into the hands of the good and gracious God revealed to us in Jesus Christ. With this settled, we turn to the question of the nature of the evil from which we're to be delivered. It is instructive that the Greek word that is translated as "evil" in this petition derives from a word that speaks of poverty and deep need. Therefore, when we ask God to deliver us from the evil with which the evil one tempts us, it appears that Jesus is speaking of actions that undermine efforts to relieve poverty and need. Or, as Michael Crosby writes:

> To pray to be "delivered from evil" involves doing good toward those in need. In this sense *ponēros* also involves economic and political iniquity, not just individual and interpersonal wrongdoing (Crosby, *The Prayer that Jesus Taught Us,* p. 165).

It's a matter, he suggests, of discerning the difference between good and bad fruit. To mix our metaphors just a bit, the question of good and bad fruit relates to the word Jesus gives about treasure. He says "that the good person brings good things out of a good treasure, and the evil person brings evil things out of an evil treasure" (Matt. 12:35). Therefore, whether it's fruit or treasure, we are confronted with the question of how we live our lives in the world before God.

The question before us, then, as we pray this prayer Jesus taught us, comes down to this: Which tree defines your life? In whom do you place your allegiance? The answer determines one's actions. Or, to put it a bit differently, what do we mean when we sing as Christians, "they will know we are Christians by our love?"

In the end the question of discernment, in which this petition is wrapped, is one of understanding that in order to say yes to God's direction we may have to say no to something else, something that may seem quite good and beneficial, but it may not be the way of God. It may not further God's desire for the world and for our lives. Shawn Copeland helps us wrestle with the meaning of this petition by speaking to the relationship of saying no and saying yes.

> In order for a no to be effective, it must be placed in the larger context of a life-affirming yes. But saying yes is not always easy either. Sometimes, even as the yes forms on the tongue, we pull back. Every yes brings with it new duties, new tasks; every yes calls up the unsettling potential of change in our lives (Copeland, "Saying Yes, Saying No," p. 66).

Saying yes may involve giving up something that seems good and desirable. The ability to say no when that is the right choice requires that the tree of our lives has been well nurtured by God's grace and presence, which involves continued attachment to God and the things of God.

Chapter Six
Sharing in God's Glory
Thine Is the Glory
1 Chronicles 29:10-13

The Lord's Prayer, as it is found in the two Gospels — Matthew and Luke — ends rather abruptly, and on a rather dark note. It is no wonder that over time a more hopeful ending was given to it. In this closing stanza of the prayer, we are reminded of the resurrection. It is a post-Easter refrain, whereby we declare our allegiance to the God who is known in the person of the risen Christ. We've come in the hope of the resurrection, seeking to find strength and peace in the presence of God. It is in this context that we hear the call of God: Lift up your hearts, lift up your eyes, and behold what great things God is doing in your midst!

With tradition at our back, we offer a bold statement of praise to the God addressed in the prayer. "For thine is the kingdom, the power, and the glory forever." The phrase isn't found in the oldest of our manuscripts, but it is a fitting closing to the prayer, seeming to belong from the very beginning. This may be due in part to the fact that this doxology, this brief statement of praise and thanksgiving, has its roots in a very ancient passage of scripture. Consider these words found in 1 Chronicles 29, which provide the foundation for our confession of faith in God.

> [10]Then David blessed the Lord in the presence of all the assembly; David said: 'Blessed are you, O Lord, the God of our ancestor Israel, for ever and ever. [11]*Yours, O Lord, are the greatness, the power, the glory, the victory, and the majesty;* for all that is in the heavens and on the earth is yours; yours is the kingdom, O Lord, and you are exalted as head above all. [12]Riches and honor come from you, and you rule over all. In your

hand are power and might; and it is in your hand to make great and to give strength to all. [13]And now, our God, we give thanks to you and praise your glorious name (1 Chr. 29:10-13).

As we sing this song of thanksgiving and praise, we again entrust our lives into the hands of the one who reigns over all. We do this ever mindful that there are still clouds hanging over our lives. We make this statement of praise without the naiveté that pretends that there are no difficulties or challenges in life. It is worth remembering that this prayer, which closes with a song of praise and thanksgiving, has a penultimate word that asks that God would keep us from the day of testing and from the clutches of the evil one. Yes, to pray this prayer with open eyes means recognizing that there are dangers abounding and that we must keep vigilant. We may gather on Easter morning to celebrate the glories of resurrection, but Good Friday must remain part of the conversation. It may not be the last word, but it is a central word.

Mindful that clouds hang over our lives and recognizing that many struggle to make sense of life and its challenges, we nonetheless come to celebrate the truth that, by virtue of the cross and the resurrection, Christ now reigns over God's kingdom. Having experienced our darkness, Christ opens the way for us to share in God's glory. May we, in response to our calls to worship, offer joyous songs, singing from the heart: Alleluia, for Christ the Lord is risen indeed! This is the good news that will sustain us as we walk in the ways of God's kingdom.

The doxology that the church in its wisdom added to this prayer may not find its origins in Jesus' own prayers, but it is an appropriate close to a prayer that calls for God's name to be hallowed, God's reign to be extended across the earth and the will of God to be accomplished on earth as in heaven. It is a fitting closure for a prayer that requests of God one's basic provisions for life, forgiveness of one's debts, and deliverance from temptation and the clutches of the evil one. It brings to a conclusion a prayer that reflects the commandments that link our lives with God's life. Having made our petitions to God who reigns on earth as in heaven, we make four affirmations about God — that God is the one who reigns with power, with glory, and for eternity.

KINGDOM

As we pray this prayer, knowing that it addresses God as Father, a form of address that carries with it the sense of patron or ruler, we understand that this prayer is a statement of allegiance. As such, it takes on a subversive, even treasonous, sense. To say, as this doxology most clearly does (even if not originally from Jesus) — "for thine is the kingdom" — would seem to require that we put any other claimant, including Caesar (or to whatever government or culture we happen to inhabit) below God and God's kingdom. Jesus may very well have told his audience to give to Caesar that which is Caesar's, but what belongs to Caesar does not include our ultimate allegiance. Yes, we may owe taxes and we should obey, where appropriate, the laws of the land, but Caesar has no ultimate hold on our lives; for God not Caesar is our provider and our deliverer, and therefore any allegiance owed belongs to God (Matt. 22:19-22).

The kingdom of God may exist in heaven, but it also exists on earth. The kingdom of God is visible, but it isn't one and the same with any human government or society. It is instead a parallel culture, where those who embrace kingdom values live life differently. In this parallel culture, the intended way of life is gracious and just, peaceable and purposeful. It is that new creation, which is marked by love of God and love of neighbor.

Although not perfectly capturing the sense of this parallel culture, we can see an expression of what is intended in the "Covenant of Civility," which Jim Wallis and others drew up in response to the angry rhetoric that had begun to tear apart the fabric of American society, threatening even the integrity of the church. In this covenant, Christian leaders from across the ideological divide committed themselves to abide by this promise:

> We pledge to God and to each other that we will lead
> by example in a country where civil discourse seems
> to have broken down. We will work to model a better
> way in how we treat each other in our many faith
> communities, even across religious and political lines.
> We will strive to create in our congregations safe and
> sacred spaces for common prayer and community
> discussion as we come together to seek God's will for
> our nation and our world ("Covenant of Civility").

By participating in God's kingdom, we can help create a different culture, one that isn't just civil, which for some might simply mean being nice, but also one that is committed to the transformation of the way we live together in the presence of God. And this experiment must start with the church. If the church can't model civility, then there's little hope for the future of our society.

POWER

Having affirmed God's reign, we also confess that God has the power to transform the world. In making this confession, I need to add a caveat. Although Scripture speaks of "almighty God," it doesn't speak of God's omnipotence. That is, while God has the power, there are some things that God cannot do. God cannot, for instance, by our confession, be good and do that which is evil.

As we contemplate the nature of God's power, it might be useful to think about how we typically envision power. For instance, the United States is considered a superpower, while China is an emerging superpower, and Russia is a declining one. When we think in these terms, power is defined by a nation's military or economic prowess. This isn't the kind of power, however, that is affirmed by this prayer.

When we think of power we usually think in terms of might and coercion. A superpower is a power without rival, and thus is able to do whatever that nation desires. There is simply no other power of equivalent nature to answer. Bruce Epperly makes the distinction between unilateral and relational power. We understand what unilateral power involves. You have the power to do what you need to do, and no one can resist. But relational power is different. Epperly writes:

> A relational God, in contrast, seeks abundant life for all things, but must work through the freedom and creativity of the world, slowly, patiently, and constantly luring the world toward greater and greater love and beauty. A relational God is not without power, but it is the power of love and relatedness, not coercion or violence. It is the power of shared vision rather than unilateral demand (Epperly, "Divine Power, Unilateral or Relational?", para. 8).

This kingdom we await works differently from human kingdoms, especially if, as I've come to believe, God works not unilaterally, but graciously works relationally. It is power, but not the kind of power we're used to imagining.

In unpacking this new sense of power, we might be well served by turning to Walter Wink once again. Wink has written quite widely on matters of power, both divine and not so divine power. In picking up the sense of relationality, Wink suggests that in prayer, we are taking the lead. We, who are part of the creation, come before God and command God to act. We do this by reminding God that God has the power and ability to bring into existence a new future and a new reality. Wink writes:

> Prayer is rattling God's cage and waking God up and setting God free and giving this famished God water and this starved God food and cutting the ropes off God's hands and the manacles off God's feet and

washing the caked sweat from God's eyes and then
watching God swell with life and vitality and energy
and following God wherever God goes (Wink, *Powers
that Be,* p. 186).

If the cross is a sign of human attempts to bind God's hands
and feet, the resurrection stands as a sign that the bonds we've
placed on God's hands and feet have been broken. The Temple
and the Empire, which tried to tie the hands of God, have failed
to finish the job. Because Christ the Lord is risen, death has lost
its sting. And God did not bring this change of fortune about by
wreaking havoc on human society. Although the Gospels suggest
that darkness came over the land at the moment of death, in the
resurrection there is no retribution or punishment; there is simply
life restored. The promise, then, is that because of the power of
God, which engages us relationally, there is no longer the need to
serve and fear death and its allies.

GLORY

Whether we turn to the description of the heavenly realm found
in Isaiah 6 or that which is found in Revelation, God is pictured
sitting on a throne in glory. The Psalms are particularly descriptive
in their declarations of God's glory, often hailing God as the newly
enthroned king and inviting God's people to sing new songs so
that they might declare God's glory among the nations, "for great
is the Lord and greatly to be praised (Psalm 96:4a).

In keeping with the confession found in this prayer that what
happens on earth is a reflection of what is also happening in
heaven, as we proclaim the glory of God on earth, it is being
declared in heaven. Yes, and the reverse is also true, so that even
as the heavenly host is gathering around the throne of God,
declaring that the Lord of hosts is holy, we also discover that the
"whole earth is full of his glory" (Isa. 6:3). Indeed, "let the heavens
be glad, and let the earth rejoice" (Ps. 96:11). God's glory is

something the earth shares with heaven, as both affirm that God is creator, redeemer, and sustainer of all things. If this is true, then we have a share in this glory. It is the benefit of giving ultimate allegiance to God.

There are many ways of joining in celebration of this divine glory, but few do it better than Harry Emerson Fosdick, whose hymn of yesteryear declares:

> God of grace and God of glory,
>> on thy people pour thy power;
> crown thine ancient church's story;
>> bring its bud to glorious flower.
> Grant us wisdom, grant us courage,
>> for the facing of this hour,
>> for the facing of this hour.
> (Fosdick, "God of Grace, and God of Glory").

This glory, of which we sing, envelops and empowers us. It does so, not just so we can face this particular hour, but so that we might live fully in God's presence every day, no matter what the situation might be. In the course of sharing in this glory, we also share in the establishment of God's reign.

FOREVER

The prayer's final assertion affirms the eternity of God's reign: "For thine is the kingdom, the power, and the glory forever." In making this affirmation we declare that God is not a human being writ large. It is true; we have been created in the image of God so that we might bear witness to God's power and glory, love and mercy. Whatever share that we might have in eternity comes to us as a gift of God's grace. Immortality is not inherent in our being. From dust we have been made and to dust we shall return, but God transcends this limitation. Eternity, that which is forever, is, according to Paul, imperishable (1 Cor. 15:53). But what is imperishable? Jürgen Moltmann, borrowing from Boethius, suggests that God's eternity means "God's unrestricted livingness and his inexhaustibly creative fullness of life." For humans, like us, eternity involves "unrestricted participation in the life of God" (Moltmann, *Sun of Righteousness,* p. 63). Eternity, then, this "forever" that the doxology celebrates, isn't something to be enjoyed only after this life ends, but in a very real way it is something that has already begun.

The prayer that Jesus teaches us, so that we might be present to God in prayer, ends on a declaration of God's infinite presence, which we have been invited to enjoy forever. It is, therefore, a word of hope, one that is rooted deeply in the promise of resurrection, for in the resurrection death itself is overcome. With this word of hope we can take confidence in the knowledge that God will be there at every moment in time. Yes, it is a promise that offers hope that we needn't traverse this life alone.

The prayer itself subverts our allegiances, but it's not a subversiveness that is undertaken just to be subversive. It's not a matter of being ornery, but is in fact a recognition that whatever benefit might be gained by our involvement in society, culture, and state, they remain secondary to our allegiance to the God whom Jesus names as Our Father.

Afterword

Over the centuries the Lord' Prayer has proven to be foundational for Christian devotion and worship. It is a prayer that perhaps a large majority of churches recite each time they gather for worship, often with little thought as to its meaning. As I have reflected upon its message, however, I have come to see it as having a subversive message. Indeed, if we see this prayer as serving as a model of Christian prayer, as well as a prayer to be recited as it stands, then prayer itself should have a subversive sense. In prayer we come to God, pledging our allegiance to the one who is our patron, our provider, our protector, and the one who will guide us into the future. As we pray prayers that are guided by this model, then we are committing ourselves to embracing God's reign, both on earth and in heaven.

As I consider the nature of this prayer and its call to give allegiance to the God of Jesus Christ, I can't help but think of other statements of allegiance that I've made in life. I may not live in the midst of the Roman Empire, an empire that demanded the worship and veneration of the Emperor, but I do live in a country that requires my allegiance. There was a time, when I was a child, that I began each school day by reciting the Pledge of Allegiance. In doing this I joined my classmates in declaring my love and support for the nation in which we lived. I doubt if I truly understood the implications of my pledge; it was just something I said every morning as school began. Only later, as I got older, did I begin to understand what it means to give my allegiance to my country. I also learned that not everyone agreed as to what this allegiance entailed. "Love it or leave it" was the message that came forth from some of my neighbors. The question that this prayer raises concerns the degree to which we understand the difference between the allegiance pledged to God in prayer, and allegiance given in other ways to nation, clan, tribe, or family.

I don't mean to sound unpatriotic or disparaging of those who
love and support their nation. I love my home country, but again
I return to the question — in what ways does my allegiance to God
trump all other allegiances? Consider for a moment those who
risked their lives in the 1930s and 1940s to hide their Jewish
neighbors or smuggle them to safety in defiance of German law.
Or consider the people who participated in the Underground
Railroad, shuttling escaped slaves north to Canada, and in doing
so broke the Fugitive Slave Law. These folks believed that there
was a higher law than that of the nation. So, to whom do we owe
ultimate allegiance? This was the question faced by the earliest
Christians, who often had to choose between their allegiance to
God and allegiance to culture and nation. In every age and culture,
leaders have appealed to patriotism, nationalism, and loyalty to the
fatherland or to the clan. Yes, even in the nation that I name as my
home, there are demagogues stirring up crowds with the words
"Let's take back our country."

Whatever our national allegiances might be, we are first of all
citizens of God's kingdom, people who acclaim Jesus, the one who
is risen from the dead, to be "Leader and Savior." It is the risen
Christ who breathes upon the disciples the Spirit and commissions
them to share the word of forgiveness (John 20:22-23). It is the
risen Christ who commissions the church to carry the message of
God's grace to the ends of the earth (Acts 1:8). It is the risen Christ,
the one who gave this prayer to us, who calls us to pray with him
a prayer of allegiance to the Father.

From the day of Pentecost until the time of Constantine, being
a Christian was dangerous if you lived in the Roman Empire. To
be a Christian was considered an act of treason, and thus arrest
and even martyrdom was common. This was due in part because
the Romans didn't practice the separation of church and state, and
so you proved your allegiance to the state by offering sacrifices to
the emperor, who was proclaimed the divine Lord of the empire.
This proved to be a problem for Christians, because they had only
one Lord, and that was Christ. So when they refused to sacrifice

and give their ultimate allegiance to the emperor, the government had no choice but to suppress them. The Romans tried to suppress the Christians by crucifying them, beheading them, burning them at the stake, or throwing them into the arena to face wild beasts and gladiators. They hoped that these violent acts would be a deterrent, but history suggests that this persecution didn't work. Polycarp, Ignatius of Antioch, and Perpetua stand as examples of those who understood the nature of their allegiance, and gave their lives for their faith. Indeed, it is an understanding of Christian faith that Dietrich Bonhoeffer captured so well in his famous phrase from the *Cost of Discipleship*: "When Christ calls a man, he bids him come and die."

As we contemplate the nature of prayer in light of the Jesus Prayer, it might behoove us to consider the testimony of the Jehovah's Witnesses or the witness of the Amish. Both of these communities have taken positions that are counter-cultural. We needn't embrace all that they affirm to respect their recognition of the challenge of competing allegiances. For a goodly number of Americans, there is the temptation to mix faith and American idealism, to make assumptions about God's special blessings for this nation. This has lead to the creation of a civil religion that is not always healthy.

The Jehovah's Witnesses have received the most ridicule and condemnation because unlike the Amish they don't gather in their own communities but live in our midst, attending the same schools as most other Americans, and yet they refuse to do such things as pledge their allegiance to the flag. Many see this refusal as being unpatriotic, but they believe that pledging allegiance to a flag is equivalent to burning incense to an emperor. It is giving allegiance to a rival claimant upon our lives. If we pray the Lord's Prayer with open eyes, what is its message concerning our place in society? What are its political implications? How do we keep from equating our allegiance to the nation with that of God? Pushing this further, in what ways does our at least implicit civil religion differ from the theocracies of places like Iran, where the separation between "church and state" is non-existent? There are those who suggest that America's laws are based upon or should be based upon the Bible. How different is this from the desire on the part of Muslim nations to use *Sharia* as the basis of their law codes?

Christians live in the world, and yet they are not of the world — that is, Christians, including American Christians, live in two parallel orders, so that the Christian's ultimate allegiance is to God and not nation, clan, tribe, or even family. When pushed, Christians are called upon to take up the stance of the Apostles as they stood before the Sanhedrin. Questioned as to their allegiances, they answered: "We must obey God rather than any human authority" (Acts 5:29). As we pray this prayer that Jesus has given us, can we along with Peter and John rejoice because we have been "considered worthy to suffer dishonor for the sake of the name" (Acts 5:41)?

For Further Reading

"A Covenant of Civility." *Sojourners.* http://www.sojo.net/index.cfm ?action=action.display&item=100308-civility-covenant.

Bonhoeffer, Dietrich. *Discipleship.* Dietrich Bonhoeffer Works, Volume 4. Edited by Geffrey B. Kelley and John D. Godsey. Translated by Barbara Green and Reinhard Krauss. Minneapolis: Fortress Press, 2001.

Boring, M. Eugene. "The Gospel of Matthew," in *The New Interpreter's Bible: A Commentary in Twelve Volumes.* Volume 8. Nashville: Abingdon Press, 1995.

Boring, M. Eugene and Fred B. Craddock, *The People's New Testament Commentary.* Louisville: Westminster John Knox Press, 2009.

Brueggemann, Walter. *The Journey to the Common Good.* Louisville: WJK Press, 2010.

Calvin, John. *Institutes of the Christian Religion.* 2 Volumes. Edited by John T. McNeill. Translated by Ford Lewis Battles. Philadelphia: Westminster Press, 1960.

Cornwall, Robert. *A Cry from the Cross: Sermons on the Seven Last Words of Christ.* Lima, OH: CSS Publishing Company.

Crosby, Michael H. *The Prayer that Jesus Taught Us.* Maryknoll, NY: Orbis Press, 2002.

Copeland, M. Shawn. "Saying Yes and Saying No," in *Practicing Our Faith.* Second edition. Edited by Dorothy C. Bass. San Francisco: Jossey-Bass, 2010.

Crossan, John Dominic. *God and Empire: Jesus against Rome, Then and Now.* (San Francisco: Harper San Francisco, 2007.

Culpepper, R. Alan. "The Gospel of Luke," in *The New Interpreter's Bible: A Commentary in Twelve Volumes.* Volume 9. Nashville: Abingdon Press, 1995.

Epperly, Bruce. "Divine Power—Unilateral or Relational?" *Ponderings on a Faith Journey.* http://pastorbobcornwall. blogspot.com/2010/05/divine-power-unilateral-or-relational.html.

Friesen, Dwight J. *Thy Kingdom Connected: What the Church Can Learn from Facebook, the Internet, and Other Networks.* Grand Rapids: Baker Books, 2009. http://www.wordorigins.org/index.php/site/comments/trespass_sin_debt/

Koenig, John. *Rediscovering New Testament Prayer: Boldness and Blessing in the Name of Jesus.* San Francisco: Harper San Francisco, 1992.

Moltmann, Jürgen. *Sun of Righteousness, Arise! God's Future for Humanity and the Earth.* Translated by Margaret Kohl. Minneapolis: Fortress Press, 2010.

Thompson, Marianne Meye. *The Promise of the Father: Jesus and God in the New Testament.* Louisville: Westminster John Knox Press, 2000.

Wink, Walter. *The Powers that Be: Theology for a New Millennium.* New York: Galilee Doubleday, 1998.

Wright, N.T. *The Lord & His Prayer.* Grand Rapids: William B. Eerdmans Publishing Company, 1997.

Wright, N. T. *Surprised by Hope: Rethinking Heaven, the Resurrection, and the Mission of the Church.* San Francisco: Harper One, 2008.

Topics and Persons Index

Scripture Index

Also by Robert D. Cornwall

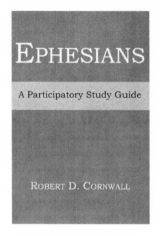

Following the outlines of the Participatory Study Method, Dr. Robert Cornwall presents a study guide to the book of Ephesians that is both usable and challenging while not skirting the difficult issues. These eight lessons take you through the letter leading from the history and background to modern application and sharing in corporate study and worship.

Whether you are approaching this book as an individual, as a small group, or in a larger classroom setting, this study guide will provide you with direction, exercises, and questions for discussion and further investigation.

Also in the
Areopagus Critical Christian Issues Series

What is the Kingdom of God? What does it mean to be part of the kingdom? These are questions that should occupy the mind of every Christian. But we frequently shy away from the full meaning of God's rule.

In *Christian Archy*, **Dr. David Alan Black** examines the New Testament to find the truly radical and all-encompassing claims of God's kingdom. In doing so, he discovers that the character of this kingdom is widely different from what is commonly contemplated today. Its glory is revealed only through suffering — a point that Jesus' disciples, then and now, have been slow to understand. This truth has tremendous implications for church life. The kingdom of God is in no way imperialistic. It has no political ambitions. It conquers not by force but by love. It is this humble characteristic of the kingdom that is a stumbling block to so many today. Christ's claim to our total allegiance is one we seek to avoid at all costs. But there is only one way to victory and peace, and that way is the way of the Lamb.

More from Energion Publications

Personal Study

The Jesus Paradigm	$17.99
Finding My Way in Christianity	$16.99
When People Speak for God	$17.99
Holy Smoke, Unholy Fire	$14.99
Not Ashamed of the Gospel	$12.99
Evidence for the Bible	$16.99
Christianity and Secularism	$16.99
What's In A Version?	$12.99
Christian Archy	$9.99
The Messiah and His Kingdom to Come	$19.99 (B&W)

Christian Living

52 Weeks of Ordinary People – Extraordinary God	$7.99
Daily Devotions of Ordinary People – Extraordinary God	$19.99
Directed Paths	$7.99
Grief: Finding the Candle of Light	$8.99
I Want to Pray	$7.99
Soup Kitchen for the Soul	$12.99

Bible Study

Learning and Living Scripture	$12.99
To the Hebrews: A Participatory Study Guide	$9.99
Revelation: A Participatory Study Guide	$9.99
The Gospel According to St. Luke: A Participatory Study Guide	$8.99
Identifying Your Gifts and Service: Small Group Edition	$12.99
Consider Christianity, Volume I & II Study Guides	$7.99 each
Why Four Gospels?	$11.99

Theology

God's Desire for the Nations	$18.99

Fiction

Megabelt	$12.99

Generous Quantity Discounts Available
Dealer Inquiries Welcome
Energion Publications
P.O. Box 841
Gonzalez, FL 32560
Website: http://energionpubs.com
Phone: (850) 525-3916

CPSIA information can be obtained at www.ICGtesting.com
Printed in the USA
BVOW031851300412

289059BV00001B/1/P